We Are Singaporeans

Volume 2

Text by **Melanie Lee**

Illustrated by **Lee Xin Li**

Marshall Cavendish Editions

Published in 2022 by Marshall Cavendish Editions
An imprint of Marshall Cavendish International

A member of the
Times Publishing Group

Other Marshall Cavendish Offices:
Marshall Cavendish Corporation, 800 Westchester Ave, Suite N-641, Rye Brook,
NY 10573, USA • Marshall Cavendish International (Thailand) Co Ltd, 253 Asoke,
16th Floor, Sukhumvit 21 Road, Klongtoey Nua, Wattana, Bangkok 10110, Thailand
• Marshall Cavendish (Malaysia) Sdn Bhd, Times Subang, Lot 46, Subang Hi-Tech
Industrial Park, Batu Tiga, 40000 Shah Alam, Selangor Darul Ehsan, Malaysia

National Library Board, Singapore Cataloguing-in-Publication Data
Name(s): Lee, Melanie, 1979- | Lee, Xin Li, 1988- illustrator.
Title: We are Singaporeans. Volume 2 / text by Melanie Lee ; illustrated by Lee Xin Li.
Description: Singapore : Marshall Cavendish Editions, [2022]
Identifier(s): ISBN 978-981-4928-42-7 (paperback)
Subject(s): LCSH: Singaporeans--Interviews. | Values--Singapore. | Lifestyles--
    Singapore. | Singapore--Social conditions--21st century.
Classification: DDC 306.095957 --dc23

Printed in Singapore

Contents

Preface

Dear readers,

This second volume of *We Are Singaporeans* was written during the second year of the pandemic. I started on these interviews feeling rather weary, but also more cognizant that these are the kind of stories that most of us would benefit from reading about during these uncertain times.

The 13 people featured here are quite different from those featured in Volume 1. Besides having unique personalities and hailing from different industries or jobs, they bring in fresh perspectives on what it means to live lives aligned with their passions and values.

Those in the performance arts like stand-up comic Sharul Channa, Darius Lim and Samantha Scott-Blackhall present the versatility of a stage – as a voice for the voiceless, a way to unite communities or a builder of worlds.

Newsmakers Martino Tan, who co-founded Mothership and Wong Maye-E, a photojournalist with the Associated Press, share their curiosity about society and humanity and how they hope to ignite that same spark in others through their stories.

Indie comics publisher Felicia Low-Jimenez and Jay Chua, Charis Chia and Yilina Leong of Fossa Chocolate, have boldly carved out new spaces in their respective industries in Singapore, but also reiterate the importance of knowing one's limitations in order to stay relentless on such challenging journeys.

Urbanist Adib Jalal, conservation biologist Debby Ng and Kenneth and Adeline Thong who offer refuge to people from their home, The Last Resort, press on with their ideals, even when reality means perpetual uncertainties.

Regardless of your aspirations or interests, there's something to learn from each of them. I'm deeply grateful to all 24 *We Are Singaporean* interviewees from both volumes who shared their life experiences. It takes a special kind of courage to be so honest and big-hearted. They are personal role models and have also shown me how I can play my part in this exponential sharing of wisdom and kindness. This book in your hand is one manifestation of this.

Melanie Lee
February 2022

p/s: If this book has left an impression on you in any way, we'd love it if you could share your reflections on social media with the hashtag #WeAreSingaporeans. Thank you!

We Are Singaporeans

Volume 2

Wong Maye-E

Wong Maye-E is an award-winning photojournalist. She started her career at *The Straits Times*, and then moved on to become a staff photographer at The Associated Press (AP). During that time, she spent about four years as the point photographer for AP's North Korea bureau. She is currently working in New York as a photojournalist and editor at The Associated Press' Global Enterprise reporting team. She has covered major world events, such as the Olympics, the Indian Ocean Tsunami, the Thailand and Hong Kong political protests and Black Lives Matter demonstrations.

I have been curious about photography from the age of 15. We had a darkroom at my secondary school and I used to tag along with my classmates who were part of the Art Elective Programme when they had to process film and make black and white prints there. Back then, I was also part of the national sailing team and I'd take my camera along to capture our travels and photograph my team.

Being a competitive sailor meant that I would miss out on a lot of classes in school. It was a struggle to balance school and sport. I knew it would be too much for me if I continued on to a junior college (JC) after the O-Level examinations. I discovered that Temasek Polytechnic (TP) offered a visual communications diploma with an option to major in photography. It was exactly what I wanted to do.

Back then, there was a stigma that people only went to a polytechnic if they could not get into a JC. However, I felt that my education at TP was so valuable — I received a foundation in graphic design and art, which helped me better understand my own approach to photography. I also had the idea that I could use photography for good. For my final year project, I worked with The Sangha Metta Project in Chiang Mai to document monks educating the villagers on HIV/AIDS prevention.

I have an intuitive approach to photojournalism. Wherever I take photographs, I try to relate my own experience and seek out the familiar. For example, when I'm in North Korea and everything seems so foreign and strange, I'd notice a mother in a corner wiping her son's face and scolding him. That's exactly what I do with my kids! While some things may seem similar, I also try to be cognizant that I don't project my own experience blindly onto others or assume to understand how everything works. Everyone is different and every culture is different, and I have to keep an open heart and mind while on my assignments. That's what keeps the work fresh. Because I try not to be judgmental, I think that's why people tend to open up to me, even those who are suspicious of journalists. They know I am sincere and will be fair and careful with their stories.

"Everyone is different and every culture is different, and I have to keep an open heart and mind while on my assignments. That's what keeps the work fresh."

The Associated Press decided to bring my skills to their headquarters in New York as part of the Global Enterprise team where we cover longer form, in-depth stories that impact the world. For example, when 700 Rohingya fled from Myanmar to Bangladesh, my colleague and I went to a Rohingya refugee camp in Bangladesh to do an investigation on women who had been raped by the Myanmar military.

While photojournalism is predominantly a boy's club, I never felt much of that imbalance nor was it posed as a disadvantage to me. Perhaps it was because of my sports background, where I'd always been competing with the boys. However, over the years, I'm becoming more aware that gender inequality does exist in many places. Some are worse than others. When I find myself in such situations, I try to focus on letting my own work shine through all the static noise. At the end of the day, I can be faced with many obstacles but if I can get the job done well, that is what counts the most.

My job challenges me in different ways because every story is different. There is no routine. However, I am learning how to remain grounded and calm regardless of ever changing situations. My roles as a mother and a photographer exist in tandem amidst these moving parts. It can be very stressful navigating uncertainty in this job where we can be waiting for a story to happen or someone to call you back. The dynamic landscape of news gathering means you have to be ready when a major news story suddenly breaks. If you top that off with needing to be decisive and a steady rock for younger children, it can be a lot. But

I have learnt not to worry too much about things I cannot control, and go with the flow, trust my gut and be present. My work and my children have helped me grow as a person because there are all these opportunities to learn new things every day.

You should be a photojournalist if you care about people and events happening around you, and desire to tell stories and document the world we live in. As I mentioned earlier, it requires you to be open to new ideas; other people's ideas. Being a photojournalist is not something you do to get rich materially (well, for most of us, there are some exceptions). It is, however, a job that will enrich your life in many other ways that are more lasting.

To find out more about Maye-E's work, visit her Instagram account @wOngmayee

Darius Lim

Darius Lim is an award-winning choir conductor and composer, and is the founder and Artistic Director of the Voices of Singapore, a charity organisation that seeks to build up a Singing Singapore. Besides the award-winning choirs he conducts, he is perhaps best known for launching the viral Singapore Virtual Choir initiative in 2020, where over 900 Singaporeans from around the world came together virtually to sing Dick Lee's *Home* as a way to lift people's spirits during the pandemic.

I started learning the piano when I was five. My dad bought me a keyboard and taught me the basics. I wrote my first song when I was seven years old and titled it, *Music*. My parents saw how much I seemed to enjoy music, so I started receiving formal piano lessons when I was in primary school.

At the same time, I was also very involved in the primary school choir and I think that's when I really learnt to love the magic of making music together with other people. In Primary 3, I was asked to play the piano for the school choir. I continued with choir in secondary school.

After my O-Levels, something rather miraculous happened. I was walking with my mum around Bugis and we chanced upon the Nanyang Academy of Fine Arts (NAFA) campus at Middle Road. We bumped into the then Head of Music, Richard Adams, who started chatting with my mother. He asked if I played the piano and when she said yes, he asked me to play something, which I did. He immediately offered me a place at NAFA. At that time, I was deciding between attending a junior college or a polytechnic, but when this opportunity came, something suddenly clicked, and I told my mum that was the place I wanted to go.

During my first year at NAFA, I was offered a place to study a double major in composition and piano. I practised hard and took every opportunity to expose myself through public performances and making use of my craft. My inspiration was my piano teacher, Benjamin Loh, who was my constant cheerleader and discipline master. He taught me the essential skills of the treatment of music.

In my second year, I starting winning piano competitions locally and abroad. At the same time, I was also a part-time assistant to my secondary school choir conductor, Joey Lye, as she led several school choirs. I would play the piano and conduct sectionals as part of my job. I discovered an innate joy in teaching choirs and found that I had a good ear for it. Meanwhile, while my piano education was going well, the rigour and isolation of practising the piano for six to eight hours every day started to seed doubts if this was the right path for me. As I enjoy the social interaction of doing music with the community, I felt disconnected from the world during such long practice sessions by myself. I remember the stress building up to a point where I started talking to myself while preparing for a piano competition in Ukraine! Being a people person, I realised that becoming a full-time concert pianist was not meant for me.

I eventually pursued a Masters in Choral Conducting at the Royal Welsh College of Music and Drama. Wales is a singing nation and they are called 'A Land of Song' for good reason because everywhere, people are singing in the streets. This inspired me to want to build up such a culture in Singapore.

When I came back from the UK, I took up the role as Assistant Choirmaster at the Singapore Symphony Children's Choir. Working at the Singapore Symphony Orchestra (SSO) was a wonderful experience as it gave me great insights to high quality music making. During my time at the SSO, I met many wonderful colleagues with whom I am still good friends with up till this day. However, after three years, I realised that what brought me the greatest joy was reaching out to the heartlands and inspiring people who think they don't know how to sing to be part of a choir. Choral music is the world's most accessible art form – almost everyone has a voice as an instrument. As an advocate of choral music and choral education, I feel that it is important to leave a legacy of inspiring people to tell stories through song.

In 2016, I founded the Voices of Singapore Festival, an annual choral festival at CHIJMES Hall. In 2018, the festival grew to 7,000 participants. This was also the year when I left the SSO in search of building something I felt deeply towards. Upon seeing the success and joy that the Voices of Singapore Festival brought to people, I considered setting up a full-time choir company. Some people thought I was crazy because choir is such a niche art form, but I felt committed to expanding this vision.

Voices of Singapore was officially set up as a non-profit organisation in 2019 and we have implemented a variety of programmes that cater to the various demographics of society. Even when Covid-19 caused many of our plans to be cancelled or put on hold, we were fortunate to have an incredible team of full-time staff led by General Manager Mervyn Ye, and teammates Dione Aw and Gabriel Ching who were able to virtualise our singing programmes and choirs. We were also very blessed to have the entire choral society — such as our board members, sponsors, collaborators, singers and supporters — all chipping in to ensure the organisation was in good stead during the crux of the pandemic. Together, we founded the first Singapore Virtual Choir project, singing *Home* in

2020. The project was aimed at instilling solidarity, hope and strength during the height of the circuit breaker when the morale of our people was low. Putting that video together required a team of 20 and we barely slept for five days, but it was the first of many projects that gave us a sense that this vision of building a Singing Singapore was starting to unfold.

These past few years have taught me that when faced with challenges, it's good to take a step back and see the bigger picture of these issues. When in doubt, do your best not to bend towards what the world thinks or expects you to do. Instead, search for the essence of what best embodies you. At the same time, while having big dreams in life is important, it is also crucial to manage expectations and be realistic about situations. Learn to pivot but don't give up. When your heart is in the right place and you know where you should be going, it becomes easier to chart your own path. At the end of the day, it's not the number of breaths that matters, but the moments that took your breath away.

To find out more about Darius' work, visit: http://voicesofsingapore.com

Debby Ng

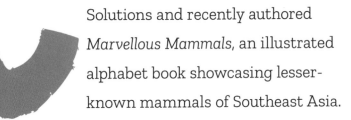

Debby Ng is a conservation biologist and photojournalist. At the age of 21, she founded the Hantu Blog, the first of its kind in Singapore. She is also the co-founder of the Himalayan Mutt Project, a programme which mobilises local communities to protect wildlife in Nepal's Annapurna Conservation Area. Debby is currently pursuing her PhD at the National University of Singapore's Centre for Nature-based Climate Solutions and recently authored *Marvellous Mammals*, an illustrated alphabet book showcasing lesser-known mammals of Southeast Asia.

Growing up, I had the opportunity to stay in my grandmother's house in Nee Soon kampong. I was outside all the time – playing with animals, digging around in mud, collecting leaves and climbing trees. For as long as I can remember, I was always curious about everything around me. This curiosity drew me to explore and observe our world deeply. The path to becoming a conservationist ran through an appreciation of the world that we live in.

When I started primary school, I had less time to play outside but I really wanted more experiences with animals. I was reading a magazine article on what kids could do during the school holidays, and one of the recommendations was volunteering at the Society for the Prevention of Cruelty to Animals (SPCA). Since it was not too far from my home, I would go there after school every day. I did this for nine years, even during the holidays. I really loved interacting with animals and appreciated being given responsibilities. Everything I know about animal behaviour and how human responsibility or the lack of it could affect them, I learnt from my time spent at the SPCA. After the animals had been cleaned and fed, I would retreat into the SPCA library where I spent the remaining

hours of the day watching documentaries and reading books about animals. I learnt that our relationship with animals extended far and beyond those of our pets; that deforestation, agriculture, scientific research, and even human entertainment, shaped our relationship with animals. I wanted to share what I had learnt with the hope of improving our relationship with animals through stories.

As such, I decided to study journalism at Ngee Ann Polytechnic's Mass Communication diploma programme. Later, I was a magazine writer and as part of the work perks, I got to learn scuba diving and received my licence in Malaysia. However, my first dive in Singapore was so bad – I didn't have a guide, was lost most of the time and didn't see anything except for one sea star. But I kept going back to see what other marine life I could find. In 2003, there was a reclamation project to extend the Pulau Bukom oil refinery to an area near a particular reef at Pulau Hantu, which was where I was diving. I was concerned that the development project would impact the reefs and wildlife at Pulau Hantu. I shared my concerns with Sivasothi, a friend and mentor at the National University of Singapore. He said, "You're a journalist. Write!" He helped me to start a blog where I would publish photos and stories about my dives. People started reading about it and some wanted to come along with us to our dives. Soon, we were guiding members of the public so they could explore this reef without the fear of getting lost or confused like I was the first time diving here. Academics also approached me through this blog to get more information on creatures that I featured in my posts. It's still an active community today.

In 2007, I received a writing assignment to do a story on the first generation of young women in Nepal who were being educated. Even though it was a month-long assignment, I ended up going back to Nepal for the next seven years to do follow-up stories on how these girls had transformed their lives and their communities.

"I learnt that our relationship with animals extended far and beyond those of our pets; that deforestation, agriculture, scientific research, and even human entertainment, shaped our relationship with animals."

My time there allowed me to develop a network and community in Nepal. In 2013, my Nepali friend, Mukhiya, a Himalayan native, invited me to visit Everest National Park with him to look for Red Pandas. When we asked the villagers about where to find them, we were told that Red Pandas are often seen when dogs carried their lifeless bodies into the village from the forest. I became curious about this behaviour and as I asked more local friends about this, I realised dogs were considered a pest. Typically, these dogs would be culled by feeding them rice with pesticide. However, all my years of experience at the SPCA enabled me to recognise that there was a more effective and humane way to address this problem. I met with village chiefs to explain how vets sterilise animals and told them if they were willing to facilitate this programme, I would help with the fundraising and garnering of support from veterinarians and friends from animal groups. They agreed, and Himalayan Mutt Project (HMP) was established.

Working on HMP made me realise that if I wanted to do more, I needed more skills and that I could do with a science degree. I pursued a Bachelor of Science with a major in Zoology and a minor in Spatial Sciences at the University of Tasmania at the age of 31. In my first year, I felt less nimble than my younger classmates. There was so much reading to do and I was insecure about keeping my scholarship for this degree, but over time, I reconnected with my purpose of being there. I had many questions and I wanted to learn to view things in new and different lenses. This mindset made me look forward to lessons. The more lenses we have, the more optimistic and creative we can be in finding different solutions.

Besides these projects, I'm also pursuing my PhD at the Centre for Nature-based Climate Solutions where I'm doing research on marine plants and how they help to keep our oceans disease-free. This centre at the National University of Singapore is a centre for excellence which advises on government environmental policies, an area I hope to be more involved in. Ultimately, I go where work is needed and where I can make things better. My diverse projects are interconnected – at the end of the day, it's really about the people. For most part, people do want to lead better lives and make the world a better place, but sometimes, we get distracted by our differences when trying to do the good work together. However, this Earth – it's our home – we have a shared responsibility to take care of it.

To find out more about Debby's work, visit
http://pulauhantu.sg
http://himalayanmuttproject.org

Martino Tan

Martino Tan is the Managing Editor and co-founder of Mothership, one of the fastest rising digital news companies in Singapore. The Mothership website attracts an average monthly viewership of over 40 million page views per month and is the second-most popular news website in Singapore. Before Mothership, Martino worked in the Prime Minister's Office as part of a communications team supporting the Prime Minister with his social media platforms.

As a teenager growing up in the 90s, I would often mull over my future. Never in my wildest dreams did I think that I would end up being a founder and Managing Editor of a news and lifestyle website.

In the days of dial-up 56kbps Internet, such a job did not exist. I did not even own a computer. But an Al Pacino movie, *The Insider*, got me thinking about a career in the media when I was 18. I was intrigued by his journalist character who pursued truth and did not stop till it was told, and wondered if I could ever be anything like him.

I was curious about the world and wanted to be involved in it. I was hungry for knowledge, especially historical events and what was happening in the present. There was just so much I wanted to find out. I began with books about history and politics. When I completed reading Lee Kuan Yew's autobiography, I moved on to books about the Kennedy brothers, and then other political leaders and major events that shaped the world.

I would have loved to take up a humanities or arts programme in a local university. Unfortunately, like

"I was curious about the world and wanted to be involved in it. I was hungry for knowledge, especially historical events and what was happening in the present. There was just so much I wanted to find out. I began with books about history and politics. When I completed reading Lee Kuan Yew's autobiography, I moved on to books about the Kennedy brothers, and then other political leaders and major events that shaped the world."

many junior college students, I did not qualify with my A-Level results. Fortunately, my supportive parents pooled all their resources to send me to Murdoch University in Australia to study mass communications and politics in 2002.

Student life in the Murdoch campus was exciting, everything was new for me living overseas and for once, I was enjoying my studies and my elected role as President of the Singapore Student Association. For our National Day celebrations, I wrote to various Singaporean ministers, requesting them to come to Perth to be our event's guest-of-honour. To my surprise and delight, Vivian Balakrishnan said yes, and he flew over for our event and had a dialogue session with the Singaporean students. This experience allowed my voice to be heard and got me interested in politics.

After graduation in 2005, I returned to Singapore and started my first job at a non-profit organisation. It was also important for me to continue to give back to society and I became a volunteer at the National Youth Council. A few years later, I was awarded a scholarship to pursue a Master in Public Policy at the Lee Kuan Yew School of Public Policy.

During my studies, I further honed my research and communications skills as a legislative assistant for a member of parliament. Subsequently, I joined the civil service and was part of a team assisting the Prime Minister in starting his social media platforms. This was in 2010 when public figures were beginning to communicate with the public via Facebook and Twitter.

In 2012, at the age of 31, I was given the opportunity to work with Lien We King to set up a social enterprise for youths and a youth media platform called Mothership. It was a hard decision to leave the civil service with a pay cut to start a media platform from scratch. Would I be able to provide stability for my family? What were my career options should it fail after a couple of years? I weighed the pros, the cons, the risks and decided to take the plunge.

In the founding years, the project had financial support from We King. With my fellow editor Belmont Lay, we mapped out our vision for Mothership – politically left-of-centre and close to the middle ground to engage young Singaporeans. Mothership would be content-driven, with interesting and exciting stories to keep readers coming back for more. The initial strategy to bring visitors to our website in 2013, was creating local shareable listicles. They got popular quickly and our first taste of success came when our viral stories caused our website to crash. We'd gotten the public's attention.

We knew we had to find our unique Singaporean voice; one that possessed wit, logic, intelligence, humour and charm. We were not afraid to push boundaries and we were willing to disagree publicly with the government and took the opportunity to be cheeky in our interviews with politicians. We definitely made readers chuckle, piqued the interest of naysayers and raised a few eyebrows within the Establishment.

Movies exaggerate depictions of newsrooms for dramatic effect but one thing they are accurate about is that the work never ends. After all, the news does not sleep during the weekend. There were times when we worked every weekend. The stress of ensuring financial stability for Mothership forced us to roll up our sleeves and do whatever we could.

Many potential clients rejected us because of our content that seemed 'bold' from a Singaporean perspective. They deemed us 'not family-friendly'. However, for the clients who chose to work with us, we helped them create their websites and social media

pages. We live-tweeted every utterance from them in conferences. We wrote countless advertorials on hair loss. Where would we be, without the trust and help from these brave supporters during our infancy?

Our turning point was our coverage of the 2015 general election which really put us in the mainstream consciousness of Singaporeans. This was our first rodeo reporting on the general elections and we exceeded expectations, becoming the go-to website for updates and reports. We did not sleep much during those 11 days!

In that same year, we decided that Mothership would transition from being a social enterprise to a proper company. During this period, many current affairs sites, led by media veterans, sadly folded.

Today, Mothership is a broader news and lifestyle website rather than a socio-political website. The team has grown to 60 employees. Our position continues to be in the centre and we are not a mouthpiece for any political side. It is important to be fair to our readers because they trust us. We owe it to them to remain balanced and give fair coverage to multiple points-of-view.

"Today, Mothership is a broader news and lifestyle website rather than a socio-political website... Our position continues to be in the centre and we are not a mouthpiece for any political side. It is important to be fair to our readers because they trust us. We owe it to them to remain balanced and give fair coverage to multiple points-of-view."

Often, I have been asked why I did not take the politician route given my knowledge, experience and interest in politics. My reply is that I am just as passionate about media and communications and right now, I am in my dream role that fulfils my niche areas of interest with my thirst for knowledge well-quenched. It is truly a privilege to be in a position to serve the public with Mothership. Democracy only works if the citizenry is well-informed, and I hope that Mothership continues to be a part of Singaporeans' daily dose of news.

To find out more about Martino's work, visit http://mothership.sg

Felicia Low-Jimenez

Felicia is the Publisher at Difference Engine, an independent comics publishing house, and the co-author of the bestselling Sherlock Sam series of children's books. She has been working with books her entire career, and was previously a book merchandiser and marketer.

My parents often brought me to the library because they both loved to read. I developed my love of reading when I was in primary school and would spend hours lost in stories. In secondary school, I had an English and literature teacher who encouraged me to pursue writing and entered my work in writing competitions. But other than that, I just really wanted to write for fun, and after school, I would rush home, do my homework, and then write my own stories.

I started reading manga and Western superhero comics in my late teens and was very interested in the characters from classics such as *Evangelion*, *Naruto* and *X-Men*. I would read about these comics online and discovered fanfiction. I read other people's entries and soon began writing my own. Some of the fanfiction I wrote was very well-received and this made me feel like a pretty good writer.

After university, I worked at Books Kinokuniya, and had the opportunity to travel to other bookstores around the world and attend international book trade fairs. These experiences taught me how the book industry worked – from how things get published to getting a customer to pick a book off the shelf.

"I had the opportunity to travel to other bookstores around the world and attend international book trade fairs. These experiences taught me how the book industry worked – from how things get published to getting a customer to pick a book off the shelf."

Later, I did book marketing and rights at Epigram Books (EB), and while working there, EB had an open call for people to write the Sherlock Sam series. The editor at the time suggested my Mexican American husband, Adan, pitch for this as he had previously co-written a Choose-Your-Own-Adventure™ book series. When Adan and I talked about it, we realised it would be better to work on the pitch together as he had only been in Singapore a few years then, and I had much more local knowledge. We pitched several stories and EB liked them. To date, we've written 17 Sherlock Sam books and sold over 130,000 copies locally. It's also been translated into other languages and sold in other countries. There's also an animated series in the works!

When we started writing Sherlock Sam, we wrote stories we would have wanted to read as kids. But the more children we meet at book events, the more conscious we are that they are very influenced by the books they read. These days, we're more careful about the topics we address and how we portray the characters. We want to be as inclusive as we can. I think our books are relatable because we're also interested in things that many kids enjoy.

When the opportunity to set up Difference Engine (DE) came up, I was working at Books Kinokuniya. I was comfortable managing two full-time jobs as a book merchandiser and a children's author. You see, I've always had two dreams – to be a writer and to work in a bookstore – and these had already come true. I never thought I'd be offered a chance to run a

publishing house and this felt too amazing to pass up. As a publisher, I would be able to publish more content with Singapore and Southeast Asian perspectives that I couldn't write about due to a lack of ability or expertise. I love learning from the creators I work with.

Currently, I'm still writing the Sherlock Sam series with Adan. Balancing that with a demanding role at DE was quite stressful in the beginning. I thought about my writing deadlines while at DE, and thought about DE deadlines while writing. I've learnt to better use my time so I can be more focused on each of these tasks. I've also learnt to be okay with saying no sometimes – I love all the work I am doing, and I don't want to dread it because I am tired.

Being a publisher has taught me how to run a company, manage a team and appreciate just how much work goes into putting a book together. While the author is usually the 'face' of the book, the editors, designers and marketing team are the unsung heroes who are also involved in a book's creation. This is why I make sure everyone is credited in a DE book. It is a team effort.

In general, the journey is going to be tough if you work in the book industry. In particular, comics have a reputation with some Singaporean parents as being 'bad' books. I think the only way we can dispel that is to keep on producing good comics with appropriate content and strong storytelling. DE is also very open to exploring how comics can be used on other platforms or paired with other art forms in ways that many people might not think about.

To find out more about Felicia's work, visit
http://differenceengine.sg
http://sherlocksam.wordpress.com
as well as @aj_low_writers on Instagram.

Adib Jalal

Adib Jalal is an urbanist whose work revolves around building connections between people and place, and breaking down complex urban issues for community discussion and action. He is currently a researcher in a think tank about cities. Previously, he was the co-founder of placemaking studio Shophouse & Co, served as Festival Director of Archifest in 2012 & 2013, and has taught in various educational institutes. He is also the creator of Urban Ideas, a community platform to share and enable ideas for a better city.

As a child, I grew up with Legos and always enjoyed building stuff and putting things together. I figured that studying architecture would allow me to continue building things and make it a 'legit' career. However, to be honest, even at architecture school, I was still wondering about my interest in buildings and cities.

In my final year at National University of Singapore (NUS), I started a blog about Asian cities and architecture called Five Foot Way because I wanted to know more about this topic. This was really the seed towards the kind of work I do today. I was getting a new understanding of architecture because I was writing about it and not designing it. Some people read my blog posts and told me that they liked what I wrote, and I was surprised by that because I never had A-grade essays in school. However, I think it's because my writing style is quite accessible and emotional, so people could understand what I was trying to communicate. Through my blog, a few design magazines even asked me to contribute articles. I would never call myself a writer, but as an introvert, writing is the best tool for me to unpack my thoughts and connect with others.

"...my writing style is quite accessible and emotional, so people could understand what I was trying to communicate. Through my blog, a few design magazines even asked me to contribute articles. I would never call myself a writer, but as an introvert, writing is the best tool for me to unpack my thoughts and connect with others.

After graduation, I worked at FARM, a studio that did not just focus on architecture projects. It also did exhibition design and organised gatherings for the creative community. This worked for me as I already knew at that time that I was interested in exploring beyond the traditional scope of architectural practice to include everything else wrapped around it. Later, I was approached to take on the role of Festival Director for Archifest, an annual architecture festival organised by the Singapore Institute of Architects. I was tasked to reimagine the festival for a wider audience. One of the things we worked on was an architectural pavilion that on the surface, looked like a fancy events tentage, but was actually created by young architects incorporating Zero Waste principles. In the pavilion, I also worked with Bjorn Low (featured in *We Are Singaporeans Vol. 1*) to create an urban farming showcase. Through this pavilion, we hoped to spark more public awareness and discussions related to bigger built environment issues.

It was also during Archifest that I met my friend Stella and realised we both shared the belief that there was a need to have people who are not architects or designers looking at the city from different angles. We set up Shophouse & Co, a placemaking consultancy, together. One of the projects we worked on was a masterplan for the Somerset Youth Precinct. Instead of a typical architectural masterplan which would be created by architects and designers sitting in a room and choosing what is aesthetically pleasing, we had a wide range of engagement sessions where we'd walk the ground with youth, and they'd point out things from their own real-life experiences. We also spoke to the other stakeholders like the business owners and other related government departments. After collecting all that information, we created a concept plan on how this space should be organised. My sense is that policymakers are increasingly more conscious about engaging different communities in the shaping of our city.

However, I recently decided to step down from my consultancy work at Shophouse & Co as the year 2020 made me rethink many things about cities and how I would like to contribute to it. One of the things I'm doing more of lately is to nurture and share ideas. This is because I think many of us, especially Gen Z youths, are increasingly passionate about how climate change and equity will affect our cities. Other than teaching, I now have a personal project called Urban Ideas where I write a fortnightly newsletter about cities and run an annual award for innovative student projects that aim to make our cities better places for our lives and our planet. I am also leaning my work to focus on broader social and environmental impact.

Besides all these, I have also been walking a lot. I walk without listening to music or podcasts, so this is the time where I can hear my own thoughts. I'm also finding that I am developing a different appreciation of the city, like how big the airport is and how there are more green spaces being carved out even as more residential estates are being built. In this exploratory phase, I'm quite content playing around with multiple ideas for now.

I would advise any young person who feels clueless to just follow your curiosity. This curiosity may lead you to topics no one has discovered or jobs that have yet to be created. In fact, I think the economy today rewards people for being different, so you should embrace being the odd one out. Your dream job may not exist now, and you may not know where you're headed, but somewhere along the way, your experiences will all add up. You may meet the right people or be given the right opportunities and things will just happen.

To find out more about Adib's work, visit:
http://urbanideas.city

Sharul Channa

Sharul Channa is a full-time stand-up comedian. She is the first Singaporean to have performed at the Melbourne International Comedy Festival and has had sold-out shows in Singapore and Australia. She has also created special stand-up performances such as 'Crazy Poor Sita' and 'Am I Old?' to highlight social issues in Singapore.

I was the kid who would be making fun of aunties and uncles at family parties, imitating the way they spoke and questioning why they were saying or doing certain things. Everyone found it hilarious.

However, I was also that kid who didn't quite know where I fit in. My father moved the family here from India when I was three months old. We all became Singapore citizens, but as a kid of colour and an immigrant student who was not very good in math (and hence, in the school's eyes, not very bright), it wasn't easy.

I studied theatre at LASALLE as a three-year diploma and was often cast in funny roles because the teachers told me I had good comedic timing but this was something I never really paid attention to. After getting my communications degree from SIM-University of Buffalo, I went to Mumbai to see if I could try acting in Bollywood. Again, I found it hard to place myself because I was not a typical-looking actress and it felt like 'making it' there would be a long-drawn process and money would run out. I decided to come back to Singapore.

When I returned, my then-boyfriend Rishi (now husband) was doing open mics at comedy clubs and I would go see him and hang out with other comedians. One day, the owner of Comedy Masala came up and asked, 'Hey, can you just jump up there and say something? No girls or locals are performing!' And so, I went up on stage and spoke for three minutes. It felt so validating and liberating to be able to make people laugh and not be judged by how I looked! And so, I kept going back to perform stand-up.

As a stand-up comedian, I have to write, produce and perform my own work. I have to go to open mics to try out what I've come up with, and perfect it until it becomes good enough to perform on a proper stage. This is different from comedic acting, where the actor reads from a script that a scriptwriter has already written and is instructed on how to act by a director.

My first break came five months into doing stand-up. I approached Kumar (one of Singapore's most popular comedians) and asked if I could be an opening act for his shows. Without batting an eyelid, he said, 'Ok, I'll let you go on for five minutes. How much do you want to be paid?' I didn't want to, but he insisted and would give me $50 after each show, even during

"As a stand-up comedian, I have to write, produce and perform my own work. I have to go to open mics to try out what I've come up with, and perfect it until it becomes good enough to perform on a proper stage. This is different from comedic acting, where the actor reads from a script that a scriptwriter has already written and is instructed on how to act by a director."

the times when I bombed on stage. During the first show when he first paid me, I'd asked him to sign that $50 note because it was a moment I wanted to remember – a very good human being was helping me unconditionally.

After a few years of doing stand-up, I realised that because it is such a personal art form, it has the potential to be quite self-absorbed after a while. I started to see writing and performing as gifts, and that these gifts should be shared with society. I decided to create my own genre of stand-up that could also be a platform to raise awareness and educate people about women's issues such as ageing, caregiving and poverty. I worked with the Association of Women for Action and Research (AWARE) to adapt their research reports into performances pieces such as 'Crazy Old Sita' and 'Am I Old?'.

Regardless of the work you're doing, if you want to be great at something, you will have to be prepared for criticism. For me, I felt that there were already so many odds I was up against – for one, stand-up comedy is typically a male-dominated industry – so there was nothing really to lose. People who talk bad about me have actually become the least of my concerns. I just have to dust it off and carry on.

My advice for young women starting out in any career is that you have to save money while you follow your dreams. If you're not able to afford your basic needs, there is a tendency to get a job that you don't want to do to make ends meet. This can cause much unhappiness. What I've learnt is that saving money also helps me to pace myself. For example, if I'm feeling burnt out or unwell, I can afford not to do gigs for a while to catch a breather.

However, I believe that there's actually nothing more important for women in Singapore than to be sure of why they do what they do and not just conform to the traditional norms of society. Keep asking: what do I want? How am I going to achieve it? And most importantly, how am I going to remain confident despite all the stones thrown my way?

To find out more about Sharul's work, visit her Instagram account @thesharulchanna

Jay Chua, Charis Chia & Yilina Leong

Jay Chua, Charis Chia and Yilina Leong
are the co-founders of Fossa Chocolate,
Singapore's first bean-to-bar chocolate
company using sustainably sourced cacao
beans. Its artisan chocolate range which uses
unique ingredients in their chocolate bars
have won awards locally and internationally.
Their chocolates are sold in the United States,
Australia, Europe, Japan and Hong Kong.

Jay Chua

I had a marketing job while I was setting Fossa up. After work, I would go to a factory space which I had rented in Tuas to make small batches of chocolate. You see, I became really interested in flavours when I was in my 20s. It started with coffee, then beer, and eventually chocolate, which I taught myself how to make. I knew that I wanted to do something related to food manufacturing and initially thought that chocolate-making could be my side hustle.

However, a large corporate order of chocolates came in one Christmas. I knew I wouldn't be able to fulfil it unless I was making chocolates full-time and so I quit my full-time job. This allowed me to think up of more possibilities for Fossa.

I would not advise on jumping into a start-up without thinking through the consequences. There's a lot of hardship and stress that comes with establishing your own business, and you need to have a very clear understanding of the business' financial state and potential.

"I would not advise on jumping into a start-up without thinking through the consequences. There's a lot of hardship and stress that comes with establishing your own business"

As Fossa grew, Charis, whom I'd met while doing marketing for a chocolate factory, joined me full-time as she's very good in flavour creation. Another former colleague from a different company, Yilina, came in a year later to handle the business development as she's really systematic. I'm more involved with production but we all help each other out according to what's needed for the business. The three of us have different strengths and make a good team.

For those of you wanting to be entrepreneurs, I think it's really important to dive deep into your business. Do a lot of research and find out more than you think you need. This is especially important in the chocolate industry, where to sell the chocolate, you have to share stories such as the bean's origin and the terrain and culture it grows in.

I think our chocolate bars with Singaporean flavours are popular abroad because of this. Our 'Salted Egg Cereal' and 'Chilli Peanut Praline' flavours do really well in the US while our 'Spicy Mala Bars' are a hit in Japan. Some people feel they get a taste of Singapore even if they can't travel here in real life. Eating our chocolate is a journey for them.

We're at this stage where we want to put out more flavours but will probably need to hire more people to find the time for that. I find it especially rewarding having collaborations with people who are game to try new things. With Pekoe & Imp (a tea business), we worked on tea chocolates using premium Chinese tea like 'Duck Shit Oolong' and with the restaurant, Wakanui, we came up with 'Smoked Chocolate'.

Charis Chia

I started working since I was 15 and at that age, only F&B businesses hire you. I was a cupcake decorator, wedding cake decorator, a waitress for hotel banquets, a pastry chef, a café manager and the list goes on.

I met Jay while I was a secretary at a chocolate factory, but I was often in the kitchen being curious about what was going on in there. Later, I was transferred to the kitchen as a chocolatier-in-training at that same factory. My family was not well-off so I was not able to go to culinary school, but I consider myself very lucky to have had people around me to teach me things. After getting a business diploma at a polytechnic, I considered continuing my studies, but once I figured out what I liked, I realised I didn't need a degree to do what I liked.

When Jay was setting up Fossa after his work, I was working in a bakery and would help him out after my work. However, later, as the orders increased, I decided to go full-time at Fossa. My experience with pastries often influences my ideas for chocolate bars.

"After getting a business diploma at a polytechnic, I considered continuing my studies, but once I figured out what I liked, I realised I didn't need a degree to do what I liked."

For example, 'salted egg black sesame cakes' were popular for a while, and I suggested to Jay that we work on a salted egg bar.

I also take inspiration from everyday foods. When I'm off work, I go around searching for ingredients to play with. Travelling is great for new ideas too. When we were in Tokyo, we got some dried shrimp and bonito flakes from the market and developed our 'Shrimp & Bonito Bar'. I'm developing a 'Kimchi Fried Rice Chocolate Bar' now and with our Japanese supplier, and I'm also exploring soya sauce-flavoured chocolate.

Yilina Leong

I studied business and marketing at the National University of Singapore (NUS) and while in school, I was involved in several food-related start-ups. To me, gaining practical knowledge of the theories I was learning in class was very important. I met Jay while I was a marketing intern and we stayed in touch after that as we were both interested in food.

After I graduated, I worked in media sales for a while and was later engaged in international business development work for food companies. When Jay was developing Fossa, I helped to take photographs of the products casually. Over time, I saw the potential for Fossa to reach out to foreign markets and that became my goal in joining the team – to introduce and develop the brand both in Singapore and internationally.

My responsibilities at Fossa are quite broad and they involve the entire spectrum of sales and marketing functions, in addition to other strategic and partnerships development work. On a day-to-day basis, I manage both local and overseas clients while looking out for like-minded brands and partners to collaborate with.

While sharing about Fossa with others, I realised that the concept of bean-to-bar chocolate is still very new to many and I'll usually spend some time on the education process. When we started a few years ago, many people thought that our chocolate was overpriced as they were only used to chocolate sold at supermarkets. Through our workshops and events over the years, we reached out to more people and over time, have seen many repeat customers who appreciate what we do. Even with the pandemic, we've gone on to do virtual workshops to continue this education.

"Through our workshops and events over the years, we reached out to more people and over time, have seen many repeat customers who appreciate what we do. Even with the pandemic, we've gone on to do virtual workshops to continue this education."

My hope for Fossa is that it will be a brand that every Singaporean knows and is proud of. Just like how Tokyo Banana has become one of the symbols of Japan and is a must-buy for travellers who visit, I hope that Fossa Chocolate will one day become synonymous with Singapore and be an icon that people remember this country by.

To find out more about Fossa Chocolate, visit:
https://fossachocolate.com

Samantha Scott-Blackhall

Samantha Scott-Blackhall is a critically acclaimed theatre director and won the Life! Theatre Awards for "Best Director" in 2005. Whilst still freelancing, she is currently the Artistic Director at Gateway Arts and is an adjunct teacher at LASALLE College of the Arts. Samantha has also worked with production and advertising companies directing and writing short films and commercials.

I directed a school play while studying at United World College (UWC) and fell in love with the process. I had this instinctive understanding of how stories can be pulled together and told and I wanted to go into that. However, I wasn't the academic type. While I excelled in subjects like theatre, music and English literature, I struggled to get through exams for other subjects. When I graduated from UWC, I received an International Baccalaureate (IB) Certificate. However, an IB Diploma is a prerequisite to enter most universities, and I wondered if I would ever be able to attend university.

In my gap year before furthering my studies, I pursued theatre as an actor, stage manager, lighting crew and usher. I was training and performing with and under the late Christina Sergeant from Mime Unlimited. It was in that year that I attended a university fair and met people from Flinders University in Adelaide, Australia. They encouraged me to apply to the Flinders Drama Centre in the school, which considered students not just on paper qualifications but their talent as well. I took the chance and travelled to Adelaide for an audition and interview. Pleased with the audition and interview, the Head of Department offered me a place as an acting student. Even then,

I knew I was only really interested in
directing, and told the school I was
only keen take up a major specifically in directing,
and would be willing to let the offer go. Fortunately,
they liked my drive and gumption on this matter and
opened a place for me in directing. Later, I received a
scholarship and earned a first-class honours degree.

Upon graduating from Flinders, and while completing
a play in Adelaide, I got a call from a production
manager I'd worked with before I'd gone to Australia
to be an assistant director for a play by Action Theatre
called *Mammon Inc*. Soon after that, I landed my first
directing gig for *Lonely Planet* by Luna-id and the jobs
just kept coming in from there. In a way, I was really
happy that my theatre career took off in Singapore
because it's where my family is and where I feel the
most at home.

As a director, I always start with the script; the
story. When I was growing up, my dad used to read
storybooks to me and my sister and he would always
put on different voices as he told us stories with soft
toys. That has stayed with me, and so I look at what
this story is trying to tell and why it should be told
right now. I start to imagine what this story world

is like. From there, I begin to think about who can tell this story well and who can help in immersing the audience in this world. I usually have a very tight relationship with the designers and actors as every element has to come together for a production to work. As a director, it's important for me to care for and empathise with the people who will help make this vision happen.

The constant challenge in theatre is making your work meaningful and worthwhile. When I was younger, I started my own company, Blank Space Theatre, so I could put up 'heavy' plays with gritty scripts like *Lord of the Flies*. These days, my trajectory has changed somewhat. I'm focusing on the next generation of artists and audiences and am exploring how theatre can tackle social issues amongst young people. For example, I worked on a production with playwright Jean Tay called *Smartypants and the Swordfish* for secondary school students, which is a retelling of the local Redhill folktale but we explore the topic of bullying from multiple points of view. I think theatre can be such a valuable tool for change, especially for youths who are thinking about their place in the world and how they want to be as people.

"As a director, I always start with the script; the story. When I was growing up, my dad used to read storybooks to me and my sister and he would always put on different voices as he told us stories with soft toys. That has stayed with me, and so I look at what this story is trying to tell and why it should be told right now."

For anyone who is interested in a career in theatre, it's important to consider your want for it. I know I can't survive without being able to orchestrate something on stage that audiences can relate to. However, if you consider financial sustainability, you may probably feel like giving up. This is why I choose to multitask – I've taken on film projects in the past and I teach theatre at LASALLE. There's no embarrassment in doing all these other things because you have to adapt and use your skills in different ways to pay the bills. In fact, I see these different aspects of my work experience feeding off each other creatively. Theatre is a very driven industry where if you believe in something, you have to push yourself to shine in that. Failures will happen but don't let that set you back. Find ways to learn more with classes, mentors and a community of like-minded people. Something will happen from there, I truly believe it.

To find out more about Samantha's work, visit her Instagram @samantha_scottb

Kenneth & Adeline Thong

Kenneth and Adeline Thong are a married couple whose home is known as 'The Last Resort', a place where young people with nowhere to go to due to abuse, sudden crisis or unfortunate circumstances can seek refuge at. Their vision is for more families and communities in Singapore to make room in their homes to provide safe spaces to those in need.

Kenneth Thong

I grew up in trying circumstances as my mum passed away when we were young and my dad didn't really know how to be a single parent. We didn't have a lot of resources so I would try to earn pocket money by playing marbles at the playground near my flat. I was a scrawny kid, and the bigger kids would often take my money away from me when I won.

Now there was this gangster, around 14 to 15 years old, who would be around watching us play while he smoked like a chimney. Somehow, I found favour with him even though we had never talked, and he would make sure I did not get bullied. This experience of a stranger extending protection unconditionally to me felt very comforting. It still sits with me deeply and I feel I'm a better person because of this.

However, I'm not really a people person. I'm incredibly introverted and even while doing youth mission work in South Africa, I was more comfortable planning and facilitating programmes rather than engaging with people. One day, a group of children were dancing together after lunch, and a five-year-old boy was standing at the side, watching. I put my arms around

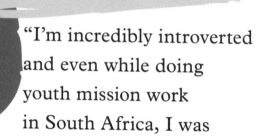

"I'm incredibly introverted
and even while doing
youth mission work
in South Africa, I was
more comfortable planning and
facilitating programmes rather
than engaging with people... I
realised that the human touch is
so important, and I began to be
more willing to share my personal
space."

him so I could bring him into the group, but then I realised he was trembling. I thought he was sick and brought him to the nurse. She told me the boy was fine but was just not used to physical affection. A light bulb came on at that moment and I realised that the human touch is so important, and I began to be more willing to share my personal space.

When friends introduced me to Adeline after I returned to Singapore, I felt that she was my first Singaporean buddy who understood and agreed with my way of looking at life. When we got married, we worked freelance or part-time because we wanted to avail ourselves to the people who came to stay with us. We never really sought out to establish anything, but word got around about our 'guest house'. One day, while we were sharing our utopian dreams to friends and social workers over dinner, someone remarked, "Oh, so you want your home to be a resort. The Last Resort." And while that was a joke, that's how our name came about. However, we're not literally the last resort, we're more like a catchment for someone who has nowhere else to go. We're not professionals, we don't have all the answers, but we're here, as a community.

As humans, we are universally wired to respond to someone in need. If someone falls down on the street, instinctively, we would gasp and want to see how the person is doing. However, it's what we do after that which perhaps needs more contemplative decision-making. In Singapore, many of us are in a hurry, and some may question if it is convenient to extend help to the person who fell. There's no such thing as a convenient act of kindness though. At 'The Last Resort', we make ourselves available in our limited capacities and struggle with the messiness and the unknown. We hope that more will join us on a similar journey to care for those in our midst.

Adeline Thong

I was six years old, at a bus stop with my grandmother who was taking me to school. A Singapore Airlines stewardess came up to me and handed me a bundle of souvenirs from her trip to London. I'd never seen her before and I never saw her again, but I remember feeling very noticed and that the world was such a wonderful place because a stranger thought of me and gave me something.

I wanted other people to experience that and my mother would tell me that after Chinese New Year, I used to cycle around the neighbourhood redistributing my *ang pow* money to other kids. Later, I would be actively involved in volunteer work as a student. It was never from a position of feeling that I was better than the people I was helping. It was more that standing alongside people is how I saw I fit into this world and what it means to be human.

When I met Kenneth, I felt I had met a kindred spirit. I had just returned from mission work in South India and he had come back from South Africa, and we both shared how welcome we had felt in the communities we had lived in overseas. When we got married, we wanted our place to be one where people could come over, whether it was for some time out, a meal or to stay with us for a while. We don't see anyone as strangers, just people we haven't met yet.

As we became known for receiving people, we realise that it was mostly young adults who came to us. There is a tendency for those between the ages 17 to 23 to feel stranded and need help because they may

"I was six years old, at a bus stop with my grandmother who was taking me to school. A Singapore Airlines stewardess came up to me and handed me a bundle of souvenirs from her trip to London. I'd never seen her before and I never saw her again, but I remember feeling very noticed and that the world was such a wonderful place because a stranger thought of me and gave me something."

still have to go to school or are too young for National Service but are too old for children's homes. Many people see 'The Last Resort' as a homeless shelter, but it's actually not. It's our home, and we invite others to be part of our family. It's a mutual thing where we all relate to each other as people and we are looking out for each other.

In many ways, what I'm hoping 'The Last Resort' can be is what I used to experience in my childhood where after school, I'd visit my neighbours and hang out at their places. Their gates were always open. While some may perceive 'The Last Resort' as our work, it's actually more about how we're trying to live life by being more present to the people in our community.

To find out more about 'The Last Resort', visit their website http://thelastresort.life or contact them at hello@thelastresort.life

About The Author

Melanie Lee is the author of *Out & About in Singapore,* a travel guide for children. She also wrote the award-winning book series, *The Adventures of Squirky the Alien,* and the middle grade graphic novel, *Amazing Ash & Superhero Ah Ma.* Besides writing, Melanie is a part-time communications lecturer at the Singapore University of Social Sciences. IG: @melanderings

About The Illustrator

Lee Xin Li is a Singaporean illustrator. The architecture graduate from the National University of Singapore sees illustration as a medium to explore the urban and cultural heritage of Singapore. It is also his way of documenting and connecting with a home that is rapidly changing. Xin Li is fascinated with the rich textures he finds in landscapes in Singapore and beyond. He uses illustration to juxtapose layers of culture, history, architecture and nature with personal references to pop culture and childhood. IG: @xinli29288

If this book has left an impression on you in any way, we'd love it if you could share your reflections on social media with the hashtag #WeAreSingaporeans. Thank you!